70/91

D0031158

SUPERCONDUCTORS

SUPERCONDUCTORS

Christopher F. Lampton

ENSLOW PUBLISHERS, INC.

Bloy St. & Ramsey Ave.   P.O. Box 38
Box 777   Aldershot
Hillside, N.J. 07205   Hants GU12 6BP
U.S.A.   U.K.

Library of Congress Cataloging in Publication Data:

Lampton, Christopher
    Superconductors / by Christopher Lampton.
        p. cm.
    Bibliography: p.
    Summary: Discusses the science, history, and potential
applications of this exciting scientific breakthrough.
        ISBN 0-89490-203-2
        1. Superconductors—Juvenile literature. [1. Superconductors.]
I. Title.
QC612.S8L28 1989
539.7'3—dc19

                                              88-31562
                                                  CIP
                                                  AC

Printed in the United States of America

10 9 8 7 6 5 4 3 2

Illustration Credits:
Argonne National Laboratories: 33, 35, 49, 51, 76; Drawing by Dennis Bailey: 14; Brookhaven National Laboratory: 56; Energy Conversion Devices, Inc.: 72, 74; Courtesy of International Business Machines Corporation: 28, 31, 41, 43, 65; Jonathan E. Jereb, University of Houston Office of Media Relations: 45; The National Portrait Gallery, Smithsonian Institution: 19; Philips Medical Systems: 59; U.S. Department of Energy: 17, 25, 61, 63, 68, 78.

CONTENTS

INTRODUCTION

It began in Zurich, Switzerland, where two scientists employed by the IBM Corporation performed an experiment that may change the world.

Where it will end is anybody's guess, but here are a few of the things that it may lead to:

•Trains that float in the air above their tracks.

•Computers ten to a thousand times faster than any available today.

•Cheap but immensely powerful magnets.

•Machines that can simulate the conditions that existed right after the birth of the universe.

•Killer satellites that can shoot nuclear missiles out of the sky.

What do these things have in common? They may all be made possible by the discovery of high-temperature superconductors.

Not long ago, few people other than scientists knew what superconductors were. Now it is hard to pick up a newspaper or magazine without seeing an article about them. Superconductors are very much in the spotlight—but what in the world are they?

To many scientists, they are the most exciting development since the invention of the transistor. They promise a revolution in the way we build a wide variety of machines: computers, electromagnets, trains, and probably quite a few other things as well.

To businesses, they are a potential source of great wealth. In a few years, the marketplace may be full of products built around superconductors. These newly discovered materials, the so-called high-temperature superconductors, may be the key to inexpensive electricity, miraculous levitating magnets, and smaller and faster computers.

To a few doubters, they are the most overrated technology of the century, a scientific curiosity that can perform some interesting tricks but will never be of much practical use.

What makes superconductors so special? They conduct electricity in an unusual way, a way that may make them one of the most important substances discovered in this century.

But that is getting ahead of our story. To understand superconductors, it is important that you first understand electricity, the stuff that flows out of the electric sockets in your wall. And to understand electricity, we will have to look at the tiny particles from which all matter is made.

1

Conductors

What is electricity?

In one sense, the answer to that question is easy. Electricity is what comes out of an electric socket. Electricity is what makes an electric light bulb glow. Electricity is what makes an electric motor run.

But what is electricity really? When we plug an appliance into an electric socket, what is it that flows out of that socket and into the appliance? What is it that flows through the filament of a light bulb, and how does it make that filament glow? How does electricity cause a motor to run?

Those questions are much harder to answer. For centuries, scientists and engineers worked with electricity without really understanding what it was, or how it did what it did. They knew that it could flow through metal wires and other substances the way water flows through pipes and stream beds, but they had no idea what was actually "flowing." They knew that electricity could make things move or make things become hot, but they had no way of knowing how it did this.

Electric Current

Because it seemed to resemble the flow of water, the flow of electricity came to be called *electric current*. But no one knew what the current of electricity was made of.

At the beginning of the twentieth century, that changed. Scientists began to understand that ordinary matter is made up of extremely tiny particles, called *atoms*, and that atoms are in turn made up of even smaller particles, which are known as *subatomic particles*. One of these smaller particles turned out to be the *electron*, the thing that electric current is made of.

Atoms are too small to be seen with the naked eye or even with conventional microscopes. However, you have probably seen drawings of atoms. Usually, these drawings depict the atom as a tiny solar system, with large particles clustered at the center (like a sun) and smaller particles orbiting in circles around it (like planets). This picture of the atom is not entirely accurate, but it does help us to understand the way in which the atom is constructed. The large particles in the center, or *nucleus*, of the atom are called *neutrons* and *protons*. They are "large" only when compared to other subatomic particles, of course. It is the number of protons in an atom's nucleus that determines what kind of *element* the atom is. An atom with a single proton in its nucleus is a hydrogen atom, an atom with two protons in its nucleus is a helium atom, and so forth. The largest atom found in nature is the uranium atom, which has ninety-two protons in its nucleus.

The particles orbiting around the nucleus are the electrons. Sometimes these electrons escape from their atoms and flow around loosely within ordinary matter, creating a "sea" of electrons. If enough electrons flow in the same direction at the same time, they become an electric current.

Positive and Negative Particles

Two of the particles that make up the atom, the proton and the electron, have a special property called *electric charge*. No one knows exactly what electric charge is, but scientists know how to identify it because of the effect that one charged particle has on other charged particles. This effect depends on the type of electric charge that each particle has.

There are two types of electric charge: *positive* and *negative*. Scientists could just as well have called these properties "black and white" or "up and down" or "hot and cold." The name given to the charge is not important. What is important is that negative charge is the opposite of positive charge.

When two particles with opposite charges come together, they attack each other. This means that a negatively charged particle will be attracted to a positively charged particle and vice versa. Once again, we do not know why this happens, but it always does.

Protons are positively charged. (That is easy to remember, since *proton* and *positive* begin with the same letter.) Electrons are negatively charged. Neutrons have no charge at all. (The very name *neutron* refers to the fact that these particles are electrically "neutral.")

Atoms have an equal number of protons and electrons. Since the positive charges of the protons balance out the negative charges of the electrons, the atom as a whole has no electric charge. Sometimes, however, an atom will lose an electron or two and the atom as a whole will gain a positive charge, because the positive charge of one or two of the protons is no longer balanced by the negative charge of the electrons. Similarly, an atom can sometimes gain an extra electron or two, and the atom as a whole will gain a negative charge. We refer to such charged atoms as *ions*. Oppositely charged ions attract one another just as oppositely charged particles do.

An electron whirling around the nucleus of an atom forms a globe-shaped *shell* around the atom. This shell is simply the area where the electron is most likely to be found at any given moment.

The more electrons surrounding the nucleus of the atom, the more of these shells there are, nested inside one another like gift boxes. Each shell can contain a certain number of electrons. The innermost shell contains, at most, two electrons. The shell surrounding the inner shell contains, at most, eight electrons. The outermost shell can also contain fewer electrons, of course.

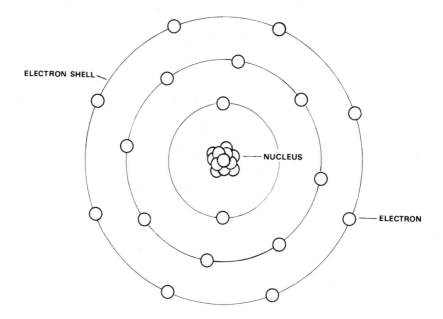

An electron whirling around the nucleus of an atom forms a globe-shaped shell around the atom.

A hydrogen atom, for instance, does not even have enough electrons to fill the innermost shell, so in a hydrogen atom this shell contains only one electron. A hydrogen ion—that is, a hydrogen atom that has lost an electron—has no electron shells at all. A helium atom, on the other hand, has a single shell made up of two electrons.

Atoms Interact With Other Atoms
This may seem very technical, but these electron shells and the number of electrons that they contain have a very important effect on the way things are in the world around you. These shells of electrons make the difference between things that are hard and things that are soft, things that are solids and things that are gases, things that burn and things that do not burn.

Electron shells are important because they influence the way in which atoms interact with one another. An atom with an outer shell that is not "full"—that is, with an outer shell that does not contain the maximum number of electrons that it is able to contain—is not stable. Such an atom will try to obtain extra electrons in order to fill its outer shell. Or it may try to *lose* electrons in order to get rid of the unstable shell completely.

The easiest place for an atom to obtain electrons for its outer-most electron shell is from another atom. For instance, suppose that one atom is trying to obtain one more electron for its outer electron shell while another atom is trying to get rid of a single electron from its outer shell. If these two atoms meet, the excess electron from the second atom can fill the electron "hole" in the outer shell of the first. The first atom will gain an electron while the second atom loses an electron.

This is a simplified explanation. In some instances neither of the two atoms actually loses or gains the electron; rather, they share the electron between them, with the electron spending some time in the outer shells of *both* atoms. However, we will continue to speak of the situation as though the electron had taken up residence with one atom or the other, which is often the case.

When one atom loses an electron and the other atom gains an electron, both atoms become ions—that is, atoms that have more or fewer electrons than they have protons. The atom that loses an electron takes on a positive charge, and the atom that gains an electron takes on a negative charge. Because these are opposite charges, the two atoms will be attracted to each other. In fact, they will tend to cling to each other.

It is this tendency of atoms to share electrons and become attached to one another that creates the solid matter that we see around us. And this tendency is a result of the way electrons form shells around atoms. In a sense, almost every characteristic of the materials that we see around us (except for their weight) arises from their electron shells. For instance, many gases—specifically those that chemists call the *noble gases*—have outer electron shells that are completely filled. Thus, they have no tendency to cling to other atoms. That is why gases, at least at room temperature, are different from solids: they do not tend to join together with other atoms to form solid structures.

What do these shells of electrons have to do with electricity? In certain substances, particularly those that we call *metals*, a large number of electrons from the outer shells of atoms are able to move around freely between other atoms. Normally there is no rhyme or reason to this motion; as far as any outside observer is concerned, these loose electrons move at random.

But sometimes outside influences will cause a large number of electrons to move in the same direction at the same time. This mass flow of electrons is called electrical current. A substance in which electrons can flow freely is called a *conductor*. This flow of electrons can be harnessed to perform useful work, such as running motors and lighting incandescent bulbs, just as the mass flow of water through a dam can be used to turn giant turbines.

What causes a large number of electrons to flow in the same direction at the same time? Usually, it is because one part of the conducting material, or a substance in contact with the conducting material, has lost some electrons, or because part of the substance has gained an excess of electrons. The electrons tend to flow from an area that has too many electrons to an area that has too few.

The mass flow of water through Chief Joseph Dam in the state of Washington is harnessed to produce electricity.

Scientists have known this for a long time, since before the discovery of electrons. The idea is credited to Benjamin Franklin, better remembered as one of the founding fathers of the United States. Although Franklin was unaware of the existence of electrons, he guessed that electricity was a kind of fluid, and that the fluid flowed from an area that contained an abundance of the fluid to an area that contained a deficit of the fluid. It was Franklin who originally used the terms *negative* and *positive* to describe the parts of the substance that had the deficit and the abundance of the fluid, respectively.

Unfortunately, the technology of the eighteenth century offered Franklin no method of determining which part of the substance had the deficit and which part the abundance. He had to guess—and, alas, he guessed wrong. But by the time scientists understood the true nature of the electric fluid, Franklin's convention of negative and positive was part of electrical theory. Today we still refer to the part of the substance that has a deficit of electrons as being positive and the part that has an abundance of electrons as being negative. Physicists have made this consistent with atomic theory by calling the charge on the electron the negative charge and the charge on the proton the positive charge. If Franklin had guessed correctly, we would probably say that electrons were positive and protons were negative. As it is, we refer to them the other way around.

Using Electricity

For electricity to be useful, we need to make it flow on demand— that is, generate a current of electrical charge when we need it. One way to do this is to create a source of moving electrons, such as a battery.

And, in fact, we can build a simple battery using a glass jar, watered-down sulfuric acid, a copper rod, a zinc rod, and a metal wire. We fill the jar with the acid and place the two rods inside,

Benjamin Franklin first used the terms negative and positive when describing electricity.

so that one end of each rod sticks out of the acid. Then we attach one end of the wire to one rod and the other end of the wire to the second rod. Immediately, an electrical current begins to flow through the wire. If we use two wires and attach them to a meter that detects electrical flow, the meter will register the presence of this current. This arrangement can cause a small light bulb to glow dimly.

What makes this electricity flow? When the zinc rod is placed in the jar, the atoms of zinc immediately begin to dissolve in the acid. But these dissolved atoms leave some of their electrons behind in the zinc, giving the zinc rod a negative charge. Meanwhile, the copper rod tends to lose electrons to the acid, which gives it a positive charge. In other words, the zinc rod now has too many electrons and the copper rod has too few. The wire running between the two rods allows the electrons to flow from the zinc rod to the copper rod, compensating for this imbalance. This *electric circuit* will continue running until the copper rod has completely dissolved into the acid.

Not all substances are electrical conductors; in fact, most substances offer considerable resistance to the passage of electrons. Hence, such substances are referred to as *nonconductors*, or *insulators*. Glass, for instance, is a good insulator, as is the air that we breathe. It is fortunate that air is an insulator; if it were not, we would be subject to frequent electrical shocks as the electricity carried by wires traveled through the air to our bodies. Of course, the rubber and plastic that we wrap around our electric wires are also insulators, which is one reason we can pick up electric wires that have current running through them without being electrocuted.

The conduction of electricity is extremely important in modern society. Without conducting wires, we would have no electricity in our homes. Electric lights would not burn. Electric stoves would not become hot. Electric motors would not run; televisions would not produce pictures; home computers would not compute. If there were no such thing as electrical conduction, the modern world would be a very different place.

There is a problem with electrical conductivity, however. That problem is *resistance*, and it is the opposite of conduction. Resistance is the tendency of a substance *not* to conduct electricity, and even the substances that we call conductors have a certain amount of it. Sometimes this is desirable, but it can also be a problem. We will discuss the causes and consequences of resistance in the next chapter.

For a long time, scientists assumed that resistance was a necessary evil. But the discovery of superconductors—especially the newly discovered high-temperature superconductors—offers the possibility that electrical resistance, and the problems that it causes, may be a thing of the past.

2

Superconductors

Why do some materials conduct electricity while others do not? One reason is that some materials, such as metals, contain loose electrons, while the electrons in other substances are tightly bound to their atoms. Tightly bound electrons cannot flow; loose electrons can. But even conductors, the substances that contain loose electrons, offer some resistance to electric current. And some conductors offer more resistance than others.

Another difference between materials that are good conductors of electricity and ones that are poor conductors lies in the structures formed by their atoms. Metals, for instance, have a *crystalline* structure, with their atoms arranged in a girderlike arrangement called a lattice. You can imagine these lattices as forming long "hallways" within the metals through which electrons can flow, like students going from classroom to classroom in a school.

Sometimes these hallways are blocked. An electron speeding through the lattice structure of a conductor may bump into an atom or molecule of the conductor that has gotten out of place. This slows the flow of electricity and slightly reduces the ability of the electric current to perform useful work. In effect, the conductor is "resisting" the flow of electricity, and we therefore refer to this phenomenon as electrical resistance.

The Trouble With Heat

The metals that we use to make electric wires are chosen for their low electrical resistance, but even these substances are not perfect conductors. A certain percentage of the power that flows through electric wires is lost to resistance—perhaps as much as 15 percent for the high-capacity wires that carry electricity from electrical generating plants to our homes. This amounts to a loss of billions of dollars a year to the electrical power companies.

The electrical power lost because of resistance also generates heat. Sometimes we can use this to our advantage, but it can also be an unfortunate byproduct.

Heat is nothing more than the motion of atoms, groups of atoms, or subatomic particles. We recognize heat as a sensation—as when we say, "I'm feeling warm" or "Boy, it's cold in here"—because our bodies have special sensory organs for detecting this motion of atoms and particles. Because too much (or too little) of this motion can be deadly to the delicate cells that make up our bodies, we experience extreme heat and extreme cold as painful sensations and tend to avoid them.

How does electrical resistance generate heat? When electrons bump into the atoms and molecules of the lattice structure of the conductor, they cause the lattice to vibrate—and this vibration is heat. In the process, the flow of electrons is slowed down; this is the resistance.

Resistance is not always undesirable. Sometimes we deliberately build electric circuits with high resistance because we *want* to generate heat. The filament in an electric light bulb, for instance, is chosen for its high resistance. It is the resistance of the filament to the electricity that is passing through it that causes it to become

As much as 15 percent of the power flowing through high-capacity wires may be lost to resistance.

hot and glow brightly. Similarly, the heating element of a stove or electric furnace gets its heat from electrical resistance.

Ironically, resistance is also *caused* by heat. When the atoms in a substance are vibrating rapidly—that is, when they are hot—they get in the way of the electrons flowing between the atoms. This creates resistance. If we could make the atoms stand still, the electrons would have a more open path through which to flow and resistance would be lowered, perhaps substantially so.

Getting Rid of Resistance

In fact, there is a way to make these atoms stand still, or nearly so. The temperature that physicists call *absolute zero* is the temperature at which all—or almost all—molecular motion ceases. (Scientists also refer to absolute zero as zero *Kelvin*, -273° *Celsius*, or -459° *Fahrenheit*.) Unfortunately, it is impossible to remove all molecular motion from a substance; there will always be a small amount of movement that can never be gotten rid of.

Nonetheless, a conducting substance with a temperature of absolute zero should, in theory, have extremely low resistance due to heat. (Resistance due to impurities in the substance would not be reduced, however.) Electrons flowing through such a substance would collide with few vibrating atoms, and little electric power will be lost to resistance. Even so, a small amount of electrical resistance would remain.

Early in this century, however, physicists discovered—much to their surprise—that it is possible to remove *all* electrical resistance from certain conductors by lowering their temperatures. And it is not even necessary to lower their temperatures all the way to absolute zero. Certain substances lose all resistance at a temperature several degrees above absolute zero. Such substances are called *superconductors*, and their very existence left physicists baffled for nearly half a century.

Superconductivity was discovered in the year 1911 by a Dutch scientist named Heike Kammerlinghe Onnes. Onnes had recently discovered a way to reduce the temperature of the gas helium until it became a liquid. He then submerged various substances in this liquid helium to see how they reacted to extremely cold temperatures, around 4 Kelvin (four degrees above absolute zero). To his surprise, he found that the metal mercury suddenly lost all electrical resistance. It became a superconductor at this temperature. He then experimented with other metals and found that many of them also became superconductors at temperatures close to absolute zero. Such substances are called low-temperature superconductors.

Scientists were quick to appreciate the advantages of superconductive materials. They could be used to create electric wires that could carry electricity without loss of power and electric circuits that did not produce heat.

They were also aware of the drawbacks of Onnes's discovery. Freezing a metal to 4 K was not easy—or cheap. If a wire had to be submerged in liquid helium before it became superconductive, then superconductivity would have to be reserved for applications important enough to justify the expense of refrigerating and transporting the helium. Such applications were not easy to find.

What to Do With Superconductors

What are some of these applications? We will take a detailed look at possible uses for superconductors in Chapter 4, but let us take a quick look right now at a few possible applications.

One is in the design of computer circuitry. Kammerlinghe Onnes would never have dreamed of such an application in 1911, of course, but today it is one of the most important areas for superconductor development.

Computer designers want to make a computer's electrical circuits as small as possible, to give the signals that move through the circuitry a short distance to travel. The shorter the distance the signals must travel, the faster the computer can operate.

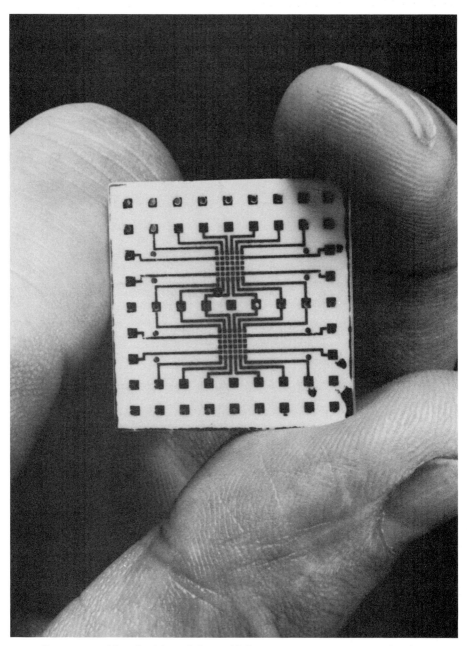

Computer chips fashioned from high-temperature superconducting materials may make faster computers.

But extremely small circuits generate a lot of heat for their size. If the circuits are tightly packed together the heat has no way to escape. A very small computer circuit would melt from the heat of its own electricity. There is a limit, therefore, to how small—and how fast—an ordinary electric circuit can be.

Superconductive circuits, on the other hand, produce far less heat. Because of this, they can be extremely small and extremely fast. But they are not easy to make. For years, the International Business Machines (IBM) Corporation worked to produce superconductive computer circuits, but it finally gave up the project as impractical. (Recent events, as we shall see, may have encouraged IBM to change its mind.)

Another important potential use of superconductors has to do with magnets. You are probably familiar with common bar magnets or with the tiny magnets that people use to attach notes to the door of the refrigerator. A magnet is a substance that produces a *magnetic field* that attracts certain metallic objects to it.

A magnetic field has two poles, usually called the *south pole* and the *north pole*. Just as opposite electric charges attract each other, so opposite magnetic poles attract each other. The north pole of one magnetic field attracts the south pole of another magnetic field and vice versa. And just as like electric charges repel each other, so like magnetic poles repel each other.

Magnetic fields are created when electric charges move. Electrons have electric charges, and they are always moving, spinning like miniature tops. Thus, electrons produce magnetic fields.

All substances contain electrons. Therefore all substances contain magnetic fields. We do not ordinarily notice these fields because there are so many of them, and they are normally pointed all in different directions. Thus the north and south magnetic poles tend to balance each other out so that the substance has no overall magnetic field, just as the positive and negative electric charges in an atom balance each other out to produce no overall charge. But if all or most of the magnetic fields in a substance line up in the same direction, the opposite poles no longer balance each other out and the substance as a whole produces a magnetic field. It becomes a magnet. This is how bar magnets work, for instance.

If you have a bar magnet and some iron filings, you can actually see a magnetic field. Just sprinkle the filings on a piece of paper, then place the magnet on top of them. The filings will rearrange themselves around the magnet in a pattern that faintly resembles the wings of a butterfly. A physicist would say that the iron filings are following the lines of magnetic force. These lines are normally invisible, but the iron filings allow us to "see" them.

Just as the spinning of electrons in a substance creates a magnetic field, so the movement of electrons in an electric current creates a magnetic field. This is the principle behind the *electromagnet*. In an electromagnet, an electric current is passed through a coil of wire to create a powerful magnetic field. An electromagnet can be used to lift metallic objects weighing many tons.

Superconducting Magnets

What does this have to do with superconductors? Quite a bit, actually. A superconducting wire can be used to build an extremely powerful electromagnet. In fact, a current moving through a superconductive coil will continue moving forever, generating a magnetic field all the while.

Something even more interesting happens when we place a superconductor in the vicinity of a magnetic field. The lines of magnetic force produced by a magnet will simply pass right through most ordinary substances, like sunlight passing through a window. But superconductors have the odd property of excluding magnetic fields. Although this sounds quite complicated, it simply means that lines of magnetic force will not pass through a superconductor. If you try to put a magnet on top of a superconductor, the magnet will actually float in the air, because its magnetic field refuses to pass through the superconductor. The magnet literally floats on top of its own magnetic field. This is called the *Meissner effect*, after the scientist who discovered it in 1933.

With the Meissner effect, a magnet literally floats on top of its own magnetic field.

The Meissner effect gives us some interesting capabilities. We can, in effect, use superconductors to make things fly a few inches above the ground. In theory, for instance, we could build trains that flew along above their tracks, by putting superconductors on the train and magnets in the track. The superconductors would be repelled by the magnetic field in the track, and the train would soar along like a low-flying airplane.

In fact, the Japanese have built an experimental superconducting train that runs on magnetic tracks, but it does not utilize the Meissner effect. Rather, it takes advantage of the fact that like magnetic charges—of magnetic coils in the track and of magnets on board the train—repel each other. This repulsion causes the train to float in the air above the tracks. Because there is no friction to slow the train's progress, it requires far less power to run than an ordinary train. Because the magnets on the train utilize superconducting materials, they have lower power requirements than conventional electromagnets, though it does cost money to keep the superconducting magnets cool. This may change, however, with the adoption of high-temperature superconductors.

The earliest superconductors would not work in the presence of strong magnetic fields. Because so many of the potential applications of superconductors involve magnets, this was a major problem. Fortunately, new superconducting materials were discovered in the 1950s that retained their superconductivity in the vicinity of much stronger magnetic fields.

A Theory of Superconductors

Scientists in the first half of the twentieth century found superconductors interesting not only because of what they could do but because no one could explain why they existed at all. Why should certain metals lose all electrical resistance at low temperatures? It was not until the late 1950s that an explanation was finally discovered by three scientists named Bardeen, Cooper, and Schrieffer.

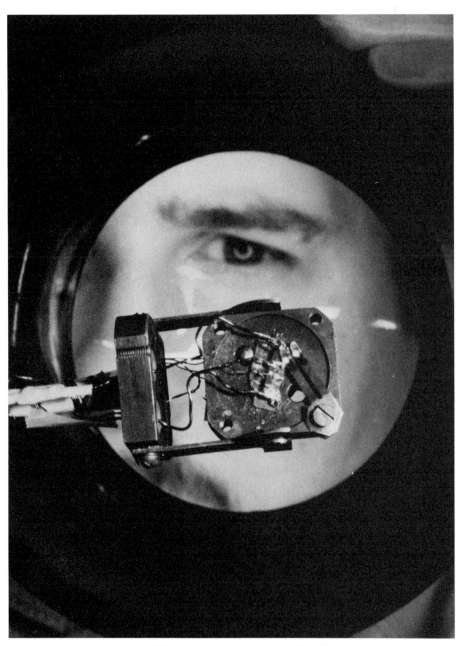

A scientist tests the ability of a superconductor to function in the presence of powerful magnetic fields.

The theory that they developed is commonly known as the BCS theory, after the initials of their last names.

The BCS theory is difficult to understand, sometimes even for scientists. We will simplify it somewhat here. The BCS theory says that electrons act in a very peculiar manner at low temperatures. They are affected by vibrations, called *phonons*, that pass through the lattice structures of the conducting substance. These vibrations force electrons to gather together in pairs, which have become known as *Cooper pairs*, after the same Cooper who was the *C* in BCS. Interestingly, the Cooper pairs act as though they are a single particle, and that "particle" behaves in a very different manner from a normal electron. Among other things, it is not deflected from its normal flow by collisions with vibrating atoms and thus shows no electrical resistance. An electric current made up of Cooper pairs flows in a different way than an electric current made up of un-paired electrons. In theory, it will never stop flowing, as an ordinary electric current eventually will. In one experiment, scientists started an electric current flowing in a superconducting circuit and found that it was still flowing strongly a year later! Why do Cooper pairs form only at low temperatures? Because at higher temperatures they would be shaken apart by the heat vibrations of the atoms around them.

In 1971, Bardeen, Cooper, and Schrieffer won a well-deserved Nobel Prize for this theory. Bardeen, in fact, was the first person to win the Nobel Prize twice for work in the same field. Some years earlier, he had won the prize for developing the transistor, the device that has made much of modern electronics, including microcomputers, possible. Can Cooper pairs form at higher temperatures? Apparently they can, but not at temperatures very much higher. In 1973, scientists discovered substances that remained superconductive at temperatures as high as 23 K. Further-more, superconductivity was discovered in substances other than metals. It was also found in a few *ceramics*. Roughly speaking, a ceramic is a substance made out of materials that have been raised to a high temperature and then cooled until they harden. Because of the nature of this process, ceramics are rigid and brittle while

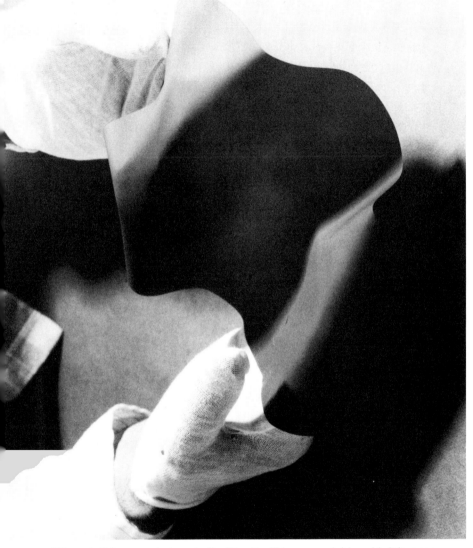

Although this ceramic tape is flexible, it will become rigid and brittle once it has been fired at a high temperature.

metals are relatively soft and flexible. An example of a ceramic would be a china dinner plate. Ordinarily, ceramics are not very good conductors—they tend, in fact, to be excellent insulators—and so it was something of a surprise to find that a few ceramics could become superconductors.

But even ceramics had to be lowered to extremely low temperatures before they were superconductive. As we noted earlier, this made it economically undesirable to use superconductors for all but a few special applications.

One of the great hopes of scientists who studied superconductors was that they would find a substance that was superconductive at 77 K. Why 77 K? Liquid helium, which is used to cool substances to temperatures near absolute zero, is very expensive and difficult to keep refrigerated. But it is possible to cool substances to 77 K with liquid nitrogen, which is quite inexpensive and relatively easy to keep refrigerated. For the cooling of superconductive electromagnets, liquid helium costs roughly four dollars a liter; liquid nitrogen would cost only twenty cents or so a liter. If superconductivity were possible at 77 K, then superconductors would be economically feasible for a much wider range of applications.

But after many years of searching, no such *high-temperature superconductors* were found, and many scientists had given up the search.

Then, in 1986, the search began again in earnest.

3

High-Temperature Superconductors

In 1986, two scientists who worked for the IBM Corporation were performing research into superconductivity. Their names were K. Alex Mueller and J. Georg Bednorz. They did not like to talk about their interest in superconductors with other scientists because, as Bednorz would later put it, "We were sure anybody would say, 'These guys are crazy!'" (quoted in *Wall Street Journal*, August 15, 1987).

In the mid-1980s, all research into high-temperature superconductors seemed crazy. Low-temperature superconductors had been discovered more than seventy years earlier, and in all that time nobody had been able to find a substance that became superconductive at temperatures higher than 23 K. What made Bednorz and Mueller's research really odd was that they were looking for superconductive ceramics.

A New Kind of Superconductor

Historically, most superconductor research has concentrated on metals. Bednorz and Mueller, however, were convinced that the secret to high-temperature superconductors lay in ceramics. For two and a half years they experimented with various ceramic substances, researching for one that became superconductive at temperatures higher than 23 K. On January 27, 1986, they found it.

Georg Bednorz had read an article in a French science journal describing a newly discovered form of copper oxide, a ceramic. Because Bednorz was studying superconducting ceramics, he wondered if this material might not be superconductive. Bednorz and Mueller immersed the copper oxide in liquid helium, wired it with electrodes, and ran an electric current through it. When they tested its resistance, it did appear to be a superconductor—and it showed signs of superconductivity at 35 K, twelve degrees higher than any substance previously discovered.

While this was not itself a revolutionary discovery—the temperature was still too low to cool the superconductor with liquid nitrogen—it showed that the two scientists were on the right track. It was now time for Bednorz and Mueller to publish the results of their work. All scientists are expected to publish descriptions of their important experiments in scientific journals, so that other scientists can read about them, criticize them, and attempt to duplicate them. When Bednorz and Mueller's description of their work appeared in a German physics journal, it created relatively little interest among their fellow physicists. This was probably because scientists had grown wary over the years of false signs of superconductivity. Many new superconductors had been discovered since Kammerlinghe Onnes's work in 1911 and some had been claimed to remain superconductive at high temperatures, but none of these had stood up to rigid scientific scrutiny.

The results obtained by the IBM scientists were not ignored completely, however. A few research teams began experimenting with the same form of copper oxide and discovered that Bednorz and Mueller had been quite correct. It was indeed a superconduc-

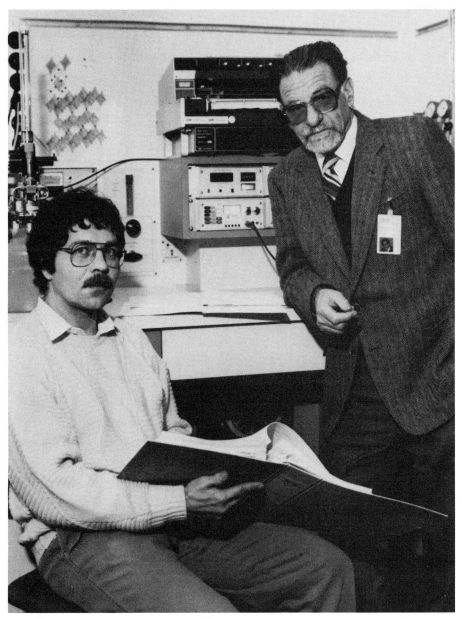

The research of J. Georg Bednorz and K. Alex Mueller of IBM's Zurich Research Facility pointed the way to the development of high-temperature superconducting ceramics.

tor—and it became superconductive at the highest temperature of any superconductor yet discovered.

Meanwhile, a team of researchers at the University of Houston went beyond simply verifying Bednorz and Mueller's experiments. They began experimenting with related ceramics, to see if they could find one that was superconductive at even higher temperatures.

The Temperature Rises

This team was headed by a physics professor named Paul Chu. Chu had been fascinated by superconductors since he was in college. There he had studied under a teacher named Bernd Matthias, a well-known expert on superconductors who had encouraged Chu to study a wide range of materials for superconductivity. At the time he read Bednorz and Mueller's journal article, Chu was also studying oxides, though not the same oxide that the IBM scientists had studied. His first reaction on reading the article was disappointment that somebody else had discovered it first. Then Chu began experimenting with variations on the copper oxide studied by Bednorz and Mueller, looking for one that was superconductive at even higher temperatures.

In an important series of experiments, Chu subjected the copper oxide to extremely great pressures, equal to 200,000 times the pressure of the earth's atmosphere. By "squeezing" the materials in this manner, he made them more superconductive. Bit by bit, he managed to increase the temperature at which the copper oxide became a superconductor. Eventually, he found hints of superconductivity at temperatures as high as 70 K!

But hints of superconductivity were not enough. He needed to find a material that would remain a genuine superconductor at even higher temperatures, high enough to allow it to be cooled by liquid nitrogen. Now Chu began playing around with the formula for the copper oxide. In the experiments performed at IBM, the two scientists had used copper oxide that contained additional quantities of the elements barium and lanthanum. When Chu tried removing these additional elements, the hints of high-temperature superconductivity went away. He reasoned that these elements must be an essential part of the formula.

But would different elements produce an even better superconductor? Chu experimented with other substances, substituting an element called yttrium (pronounced "ih-tree-um") for the lanthanum. The yttrium did the trick. He cooled the new ceramic to 90 K, and its electrical resistance plunged. It became a superconductor! Furthermore, it became a superconductor at such a high temperature that it could easily be cooled by liquid nitrogen!

As shown on the computer graph, a sudden drop in electrical resistance indicates the presence of superconductivity.

It was late January 1987. Chu realized that he had just made one of the biggest scientific discoveries of the decade, if not the century. It was quite possible that he could win a Nobel Prize for his research. (Indeed, the IBM scientists Bednorz and Mueller would win the 1987 Nobel Prize in physics for their work.) It might also prove to be a commercially important discovery: there was money in superconductors. Somewhat hesitantly, Chu made the announcement of his discovery at a scientific meeting a few days later, but he withheld some important information. He did not tell the other scientists exactly how to make the superconducting ceramic.

Superconductor Mania

The results were predictable. The scientific world went into a frenzy. Anybody who was remotely involved in superconductor research started searching for the secret of Chu's new superconductor—but they could not find it. All they knew was that it was a form of copper oxide and that it probably contained other elements as well. But what were the other elements?

Chu decided to publish the results of his experiment in the publication *Physical Review Letters. Physical Review Letters* is one of the most respected journals in the science of physics, and it is very widely read.

Once Chu's results (and the formula for his superconductor) were published, in March of 1987, scientists around the world began working frantically to duplicate it and produce even better superconductors. Laboratories competed against other laboratories to produce the best superconductors and laboratories in the United States competed against laboratories in Japan, where interest in superconductors is also high.

The next major goal in superconductor research was *room-temperature superconductors*, materials that were superconductive under normal conditions. While nitrogen-cooled superconductors

Dr. Paul Chu discovered high-temperature superconductors—materials that lose all electrical resistance at temperatures higher than 77 K, the temperature of liquid nitrogen.

opened possible applications that had not existed with helium-cooled superconductors, room-temperature superconductors would produce more applications still because they would not need to be refrigerated at all. In fact, room-temperature superconductors could all but replace normal conductors for electric wiring, electronic circuitry, and everything else that required conduction of electrons.

At the end of March, a conference was held among scientists that has been called "the Woodstock of physics," after the famous rock music concert of the late 1960s. From descriptions of the event in news magazines, it does indeed sound as much like a rock concert as a scientific conference, with physicists fighting each other for a chance to hear researchers give their reports on new superconducting materials. The presentations on superconductivity lasted from six in the evening until three in the morning.

At this landmark meeting—and, indeed, in the months that followed—report followed report of new breakthroughs in superconductivity. One experimenter after another found hints of superconductivity at higher and higher temperatures. But hints of superconductivity were not the same thing as superconductivity.

Here are a few samples of the news items that followed the March publication of Chu's paper:

In April 1987, a research group at Wayne State University in Detroit announced that they had discovered a form of copper oxide that showed signs of superconductivity at a temperature of 240 K, the equivalent of -27° F (-33° C). This is hardly room temperature, but it is not outside the normal range of temperatures encountered during, say, a Canadian winter. Unfortunately, the material was not fully superconductive. The "sign," or indication, of superconductivity noted by the team was the *Josephson effect*, a phenomenon in which an electric current passing through the substance produces radio waves (or vice versa). The effect is named after the British physicist Brian Josephson, who discovered it in 1962. No one is sure whether the Josephson effect observed by the team is a sign of true superconductivity. For that, further observations will be necessary.

Later that month, the Toshiba Corporation of Japan announced the discovery of a material that became superconductive at 100 K. This is no more than 10 K above Paul Chu's previous record and nowhere near the temperatures claimed by Wayne State, but the evidence for superconductivity in the Toshiba substance is much more persuasive than that offered by the Wayne State team.

By the time June arrived, a Michigan company called Energy Conversion Devices announced that they had tested a material that showed signs of superconductivity at temperatures as high as 90° F (32° C or 310 K)! If true, this would be a genuine room-temperature superconductor. Unfortunately, the material shows only fleeting signs of superconductivity. Specifically, it was shown occasionally to exclude a magnetic field. The material will need considerably more refining before it will be useful for applications as a room-temperature superconductor.

In the fall of the year, the most astonishing report of all appeared, but by this time scientists were so numbed by the barrage of discoveries that it caused much less excitement than it would have a year earlier. Ahmed Erbil of the Georgia Institute of Technology detected signs of superconductivity at 440 K (227° C), higher than the boiling point of water. But the sign of superconductivity that Erbil had seen was merely an unexpected drop in electrical resistance, not the absence of that resistance. In fact, there is no evidence that what Erbil discovered will ever have any practical use, though future discoveries may prove otherwise.

The Next Step
By the end of 1987, then, the record for true superconductivity still stood at 93 K. Physicists began to wonder if this temperature didn't represent an upper limit for superconductivity. Perhaps true room-temperature superconductivity—superconductors that would remain

superconductive without special refrigeration—would never be achieved.

Then, in early 1988, a new wave of discoveries began, featuring a brand-new breed of superconductors. The type of superconductor discovered by Paul Chu is sometimes referred to as a 1-2-3 compound, because its chemical formula is $Y_1Ba_2Cu_3O_7$. (This means that it contains one atom of yttrium, or Y, for every two atoms of barium, or Ba, every three atoms of copper, or Cu, and every seven atoms of oxygen, or O.) These new superconductors discovered by an IBM scientist and his colleagues contain either the element bismuth or a new form of a thallium-based element in place of yttrium. They have been dubbed the "triple-digit" superconductors because they become superconductive at temperatures above 100 K (that is, temperatures with three digits in them).

A team of Japanese researchers, headed by physicist Hiroshi Maeda, announced on January 22, 1988, that they had discovered a bismuth-based compound that showed signs of superconductivity at 120 K and became a true superconductor at 110 K. Three days later, Paul Chu and his team at the University of Houston confirmed these results.

On February 15, 1988, Allen Hermann of the University of Arkansas announced the discovery of a superconducting compound based on thallium rather than bismuth. This compound became a superconductor at 103 K, though it began showing signs of superconductivity as high as 123 K.

At a conference on superconductors held in Interlaken, Switzerland, in early March 1988, a scientist from IBM's Almaden Research Laboratory in California announced that his colleagues had discovered another form of the new thallium-based superconductor that became a true superconductor at 118 K. Before the conference was over, the IBM scientists had pushed the *transition temperature* of their compound—the temperature at which it becomes superconductive—as high as 125 K. As of this writing, this

High-Temperature Superconductor

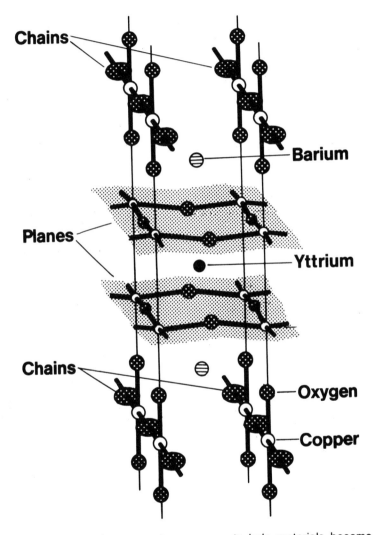

Chains of copper and oxygen atoms appear to help materials become superconductive at high temperatures.

temperature remains the record. Many scientists, however, believe that still higher transition temperatures will be found. Paul Chu believes that room-temperature superconductors are a very real possibility.

In addition, brand-new types of high-temperature superconductors have been found. AT&T's Bell Laboratories has produced a superconductor that does not contain copper, an essential element in earlier ceramic superconductors—and one that was considered essential for the superconducting phenomenon in this type of material. A team at the University of Tokyo has discovered superconductivity in an organic salt—a carbon-based compound—with a transition temperature of 10.4 K. Although this transition temperature is low compared to some recently discovered superconductors, it is exciting because it indicates that the best types of superconductors may be types of compounds that have not yet been examined for superconductivity. The possibilities for new superconductive materials are almost literally endless.

One of the most interesting, and unexpected, would be the development of a superconducting polymer—a plastic that can conduct electricity without resistance. Though no such polymers have been discovered to date, a team of researchers at the BASF Plastic Research Laboratory in West Germany has developed plastics that do conduct electricity. The discovery of a superconducting polymer would have tremendous implications for practical superconductor applications, as we shall see in the last chapter of this book.

A New Theory?

According to the BCS theory, superconductivity is the result of so-called Cooper pairs forming under the influence of phonon vibrations in an atomic lattice. But these pairs were believed to shake apart at temperatures higher than about 20 K. What, then, is the explanation for these new high-temperature superconductors?

Scientists test new substances for superconductivity by running electricity through them.

Nobody is quite sure yet, but scientists are eager to find out. If an explanation of high-temperature superconductors can be uncovered, then new compounds can be custom-tailored to be superconductive at high temperatures. And if the theory allows for room-temperature superconductors, then physicists may begin manufacturing them soon.

But what might the explanation be? Physicists are not yet willing to give up the idea that Cooper pairs are responsible for superconductivity, but it is unlikely that the pairs are held together by phonon vibrations in high-temperature superconductors. Other mysterious vibrations and forces have been proposed, with catchy names such as excitons, spinons, holons, and magnons, but none have been verified as the cause of high-temperature superconductivity.

The new triple-digit compounds have caused tremendous excitement, however, because of the structure of their molecules. On an atomic level, they consist of layers of copper and oxygen atoms sandwiched between layers of bismuth (or thallium, depending on the type of compound). Interestingly, the more layers of copper and oxygen between the layers of bismuth or thallium, the higher the transition temperature is! Does this mean that physicists can create room-temperature superconductors simply by sandwiching more layers of copper and oxygen between the thallium/bismuth layers? Probably not. Most physicists believe that there will be a point of diminishing returns, that is, a limit to how many additional layers of copper and oxygen can produce higher transition temperatures. Paul Grant, of the IBM Almaden Research Center, believes that the limit for the thallium compounds will probably be about 200 K. The limit for the bismuth compounds, which tend to have lower transition temperatures than the thallium compounds, will probably not be as high. Still, compounds using other elements in place of thallium and bismuth may have even higher transition temperatures.

4

Superconductor
Applications

Now that we have discovered high-temperature superconductors, what are we going to do with them?

Anything that involves the movement of electrons, be it electric power transmission, electronic information processing, or electromagnetism, can be done more efficiently using superconductive materials. And yet relatively little commercial use has been made of superconductors in the nearly eighty years since their discovery. The reason, of course, is that low-temperature superconductors—the only kind available until early 1987—are expensive and awkward to use. They must be refrigerated to temperatures very near absolute zero, using liquid helium. This refrigeration requires a lot of money and a lot of effort. Most potential applications for superconductors simply aren't worth that effort.

For instance, an electric company might be able to save about twenty million dollars worth of power each year that would otherwise have been lost to electrical resistance by using superconductive cables to carry electricity to consumers. But if it cost thirty million dollars to refrigerate and otherwise maintain these superconductive cables, the result would be a net loss of ten million dollars to the power company. It just wouldn't be worth the expense.

To take another example, a personal computer based on super-conducting circuits might perform calculations a hundred or even a thousand times faster than a personal computer based on conventional electronics. Such a computer would be very attractive for business or home use. But if it cost a hundred times as much as a conventional personal computer because of the expensive equipment required to keep the superconductors cold, and if the refrigeration unit was so large that the computer would no longer sit on a desktop, then no one would buy it. A computer company would be foolish to develop such a computer.

High Temperatures are Cheaper

With the development of high-temperature superconductors—that is, superconductors with transition temperatures above 100 K, so that they can be cooled with liquid nitrogen—the upkeep on super-conductive circuits becomes a great deal less expensive. Power companies will now begin to look seriously at the possibility of delivering power through superconducting wires. Computer companies might seriously consider building a few superconducting personal computers, though they would probably still be quite expensive. The introduction of high-temperature superconductors changes the rules of the superconductor game.

And if room-temperature superconductors are developed, there will be no extra expense at all for maintaining superconducting circuits. Such circuits will not need to be refrigerated. It may be feasible to replace all existing wiring and circuitry with superconducting materials. Ultrafast personal computers based on superconductors will be no more expensive than today's personal computers. Power companies will replace all of their wiring with superconducting wires.

Thus, we can break down the history of superconductors into

three phases: low-temperature superconducting (requiring temperatures near absolute zero), high–temperature superconducting (requiring temperatures below room temperature but considerably higher than absolute zero), and room-temperature superconducting. The second of these phases has just begun. The third may never happen, though some scientists believe that it is just around the corner.

Let us look at a handful of superconductor applications that may or may not become reality in the next few years. Most of these applications (unless noted otherwise) were not feasible with low-temperature superconductors, because of the tremendous expense involved; some of them have become feasible now that high–temperature superconductors are available; more than a few of them will have to await the discovery of room-temperature superconductors.

Power Systems

Not only do ordinary power lines lose a great deal of power to electrical resistance, but they are limited in how far they can carry electricity. The longer the line, the greater the resistance. Thus, it is more economical for power companies to build multiple power plants in different places across the United States and send that power over local lines than to build large central stations and send power for many hundreds or thousands of miles.

With superconducting wires, the entire North American continent could be joined in a transcontinental power grid. If one station failed, it could bring in power from other stations thousands of miles distant as a backup, through superconducting wires that might well run underground. It would also allow the introduction of power into remote parts of the world where living conditions are still relatively primitive. Nuclear reactors and other forms of power generation that can release dangerous substances in the air could be placed far from populated areas. And we would finally be able to utilize power resources that were once too remote to be useful for electrical generation, such as the powerful rivers of northern Canada.

Electric motors, which operate by producing magnetic fields that cause turbines to spin, would be much more efficient. When motors are made more efficient, the fuel that runs the motors will

Superconducting electric cables may one day make it possible to transmit large amounts of electric power over long distances with a minimal loss of energy.

be used more efficiently. Valuable resources of petroleum and natural gas will dwindle more slowly.

Electric automobiles may even become a realistic possibility. In the past, the idea of running cars on electricity was largely ignored, because there was no way to store enough electricity or use it efficiently enough to allow such cars to travel as far as gasoline-powered vehicles. But cars with superconducting electrical devices inside them would run more efficiently and could store electric power in coils of superconducting wire, giving them a considerable distance advantage. Unfortunately, this is an application that will probably need to wait for room-temperature superconductivity, since it is unlikely that anyone would buy a car that needed to lug around large supplies of liquid nitrogen.

Computers

The Josephson effect, which we mentioned in the last chapter, is an odd quirk of subatomic particle behavior. Research at AT&T's Bell Laboratories has suggested that computer circuit designers could take advantage of this quirk by making circuits out of a thin layer of insulating material sandwiched between two superconductive layers. Because of the Josephson effect, electrons would jump from one superconductive layer to the other, without ever touching the insulator. Such *Josephson junctions* are very fast; in theory, these circuits could be used to build computers much faster than any in operation today. But, using ordinary low-temperature superconductors, a computer based on JJ chips (as they are sometimes called) must be cooled with liquid helium before they become operative. With the new superconductors, on the other hand, such computers would be much less expensive to develop and use.

The IBM Corporation was involved in Josephson junction computer research for fourteen years before giving it up in 1983 as an unworkable idea. Now interest in JJ chips has been revived, and many companies, possibly including IBM, will become involved in their production. In fact, one of the scientists involved in Josephson junction research at IBM left that company when the project was canceled and founded a new company called Hypres. In 1987 Hypres announced its first product, an oscilloscope that uses JJ chips based on low-temperature superconductors. At that point, no product was being sold which used high-temperature superconductors. (An oscilloscope is a televisionlike device used to study the activity of electrons inside electrical circuitry.)

If room-temperature superconductivity becomes a reality, Josephson junctions and other compact, high-speed superconducting circuits may become common even in home computers. Such a computer might be as powerful as the so-called supercomputers of today. The chips that they contain may be small enough so that trillions of bytes (characters) of memory could be packed inside the computer's case. You would have the equivalent of a library of books available at the touch of a key, along with every computer game ever written, if such was your fancy. Animation on such a computer would be more realistic than television, allowing you to play games so stunningly vivid that they might seem more like real-life experiences. And a superconducting computer might be small enough for you to carry it to school in your lunch bag (though you might have to leave the color monitor at home).

Nuclear Magnetic Resonance (NMR)

Nuclear magnetic resonance (NMR) is a method of viewing the inside of a human body, similar but not identical to X-rays. Also known in the medical world as *magnetic resonance imaging* (MRI), NMR uses a magnetic field to cause certain atoms within the body to create bursts of energy. These bursts of energy can be detected by sensitive instruments and used to map living tissue and the fluids that flow through them.

Among other things, this method can be used to trace the way blood flows through arteries and veins. It can help to predict whether a person is likely to have a stroke or other problems involving blood flow to the brain. It can also spot artery disease, where an artery may be blocked and the flow of blood slowed down.

Because NMR does not use X-rays, it does not expose the patient to dangerous radiation. Neither does it involve any kind of surgery.

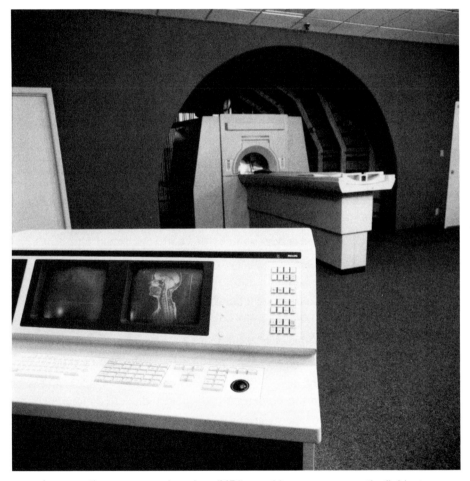

A magnetic resonance imaging (MRI) machine uses magnetic fields to examine the internal tissues of the human body.

Because NMR uses powerful magnetic fields, it is an ideal application for superconducting magnets. In fact, there are already NMR systems based around low-temperature superconductors. In the future, high-temperature superconductors, or even the hypothetical room-temperature superconductors, may allow relatively inexpensive NMR systems to be built. These systems would be affordable by small hospitals that cannot currently utilize this technology.

Nuclear Fusion

During the energy crisis of the 1970s, when oil and gasoline became hard to get and the price of fuel rocketed sky-high, scientists accelerated the search for new sources of energy, alternatives to the fossil fuels (such as oil and natural gas) that were being quickly exhausted. Now the energy crisis is over, but only temporarily. At the rate we are using fossil fuels today, we will be lucky if supplies last very far into the next century—the century in which you will be spending much of your life. Furthermore, the burning of fossil fuels pollutes the atmosphere, degrading the quality of life. It is still important that new sources of energy be found and utilized.

One source that seemed promising after the Second World War was nuclear fission, which generated energy through the "splitting" of uranium and plutonium atoms. But fission, the source of power at nuclear power plants, has a number of drawbacks. It produces dangerous radioactive wastes that are difficult to dispose of safely. There is the looming possibility of nuclear accidents, such as the one at Chernobyl in the Soviet Union, where radioactive materials are released directly into the atmosphere. And the supply of uranium fuel for these plants is currently vanishing as rapidly as fossil fuels; unless new ways of generating nuclear energy are found soon, it will be insufficient to keep up with our growing energy needs.

One possible alternative is *nuclear fusion*, which produces energy by ramming hydrogen atoms together at high speeds, fusing them into atoms of helium. This process releases even greater quantities of energy than nuclear fission and does not produce dangerous radioactive byproducts, but no one has successfully produced a working fusion reactor.

The problem lies in our ability to keep hydrogen gas "bottled up" while we raise its temperature to a level sufficient to cause violent collisions between the atoms. If we trapped the atoms in a physical bottle—one of glass or metal, for instance—the atoms would be cooled off by the unheated bottle as rapidly as they were heated by the laser beams that scientists use to raise their temperature. Alternatively, if we heated the bottle, it would vaporize into

Scientists study how to design practical, working fusion reactors.

a hot gas itself. The secret, according to most researchers, is to trap the hydrogen atoms in a *magnetic bottle*—that is, a "bottle" made out of a powerful magnetic field. The hydrogen ions in the gas would be trapped in this field as surely as iron filings are caught up in the magnetic field around a bar magnet.

But powerful magnets are not easy to build or to keep running. Huge amounts of electricity are needed to power the electromagnets that create the magnetic bottle. The solution? It might well be superconductors, which can be used quite inexpensively to generate powerful magnetic forces around a coiled wire. Superconductive electromagnets may play an important role in the development of what could turn out to be the most significant energy source of the twenty-first century.

This is one application that is important enough to justify the use of refrigeration units to keep low-or high-temperature superconductors cooled to their transition temperatures. By the time working fusion reactors have been developed, however, room-temperature superconductors may well be available.

Flying Trains

Trains that float above magnetic tracks are called *maglevs*, short for "magnetic levitation." At the present time, most work on maglevs is being done in Europe and Japan. Maglevs based on low-temperature superconductors already exist in the form of experimental demonstration models, but they are very expensive to operate and for that reason have not been very successful. The Japanese have built a maglev that runs at speeds as high as 300 miles per hour (480 kilometers per hour), making it easily the fastest train in the world, and probably the fastest form of ground transportation other than experimental racecars. Maglevs have the potential to revolutionize everyday transportation. A commuter who took a nonstop maglev to work in the morning could live in Washington, D.C., and work in New York City (or vice versa) without spending any more time getting to work than the average big-city commuter.

Nonetheless, maglevs are expensive to build for other reasons as well, so you may not see one in your home town any time soon. Still, it is an exciting technology and one of the most dramatic applications of superconductors.

Star Wars
Han Solo's spaceship may not have been equipped with superconducting circuitry (though R2-D2's brain probably was), but the scientists who are designing the *Strategic Defense Initiative* (SDI; nicknamed "Star Wars") have some superconductor applications in

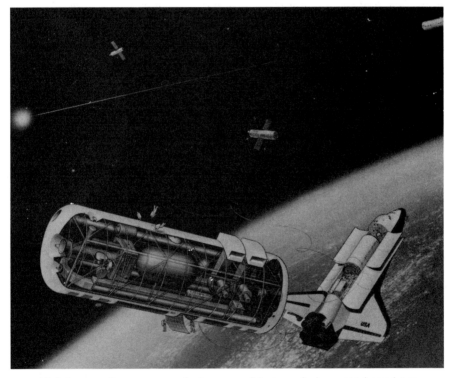

High-temperature superconductors may have a role in space-based particle beam weapons.

mind. SDI is the project initiated by former President Ronald Reagan to build a defense against nuclear weapons based largely in satellites orbiting the earth.

One type of weapon proposed for the SDI defense is the *particle beam weapon*, or PBW. A PBW fires subatomic particles at nuclear missiles in an attempt to scramble their guidance circuitry and make them crash. To do this, however, it must first get a "grip" on the particles. The designers of PBWs would like to do this with magnets, which could grip charged particles with magnetic fields.

But what kind of magnet should be used? To minimize the amount of power used and maximize the "kick" of the weapon, superconducting magnets would be best. But keeping a superconductor cool in orbit is a tricky problem. Space is cold, but the unshielded heat of the sun is intense—and the PBW would probably generate quite a bit of heat of its own. Thus, high-temperature superconductors, which could withstand this heat, may have a role in the weapons of the future.

The SDI defense is quite controversial. There are many people who argue that it will not work, that it may even increase the dangers of nuclear destruction. Nonetheless, the military may be the first part of society to make large-scale use of the new high-temperature superconductors, simply because it is well funded and can afford to perform the necessary research and development that will make superconductor applications real.

SQUIDs

No, these are not relatives of the octopus; *SQUID* is short for *superconducting quantum interference device*. It is a type of *magnetometer*, a device for measuring the strength of very small magnetic fields. They are used in various kinds of scientific studies, as well as in medical research and diagnosis. SQUIDs are based on Josephson junctions. They can be made very sensitive to weak magnetic fields. SQUIDs can also be made extremely small, until

Seen here magnified more than 500 times, a SQUID can be used for extremely sensitive magnetic measurements–even of the tiny magnetic fields caused by electrical currents in the human brain.

they are practically microscopic. Possible applications of high-temperature superconductor SQUIDs include devices that can be slipped over a person's head to measure the electrical signals that travel through brain cells, allowing scientists to study the way in which the brain works. SQUIDs based on low-temperature superconductors are already commercially available.

Atom Smashers

Much of the important work of twentieth-century physics, particularly the search for the fundamental particles of which matter is made, has been done with the aid of *particle accelerators*, also known as atom smashers, supercolliders, and cyclotrons. These machines accelerate subatomic particles to very high speeds, then steer them into violent collisions with one another through the assistance of powerful electromagnets.

What good does that do? When two or more particles collide at a high speed, a certain amount of their energy is transformed into matter, according to Albert Einstein's famous equation $E=mc^2$ (where E equals the amount of energy, m the amount of matter, and c the speed of light). Out of the collision comes a bevy of brand-new particles, none of which had previously existed. Physicists have discovered literally dozens of new subatomic particles in this manner, some of which they had never suspected existed, some of which had been predicted in advance.

These particles tell physicists much about the ultimate nature of subatomic particles—and of the universe itself. Recently, physicists have realized that the birth of the universe—the so-called Big Bang explosion in which all of the stars, galaxies, and planets were created—was itself a kind of giant particle accelerator. In the first few moments after that explosion, the universe was extremely dense, with a tremendous amount of energy packed into a relatively small volume of space. Particles collided constantly with other particles. Energy changed constantly into matter and matter into energy.

Needless to say, the universe was very different then from the way it is now. But if we can understand what the universe was like in those first few seconds, we can gain crucial insights into why the universe is the way it is now; perhaps we can even learn why the universe exists, and why *we* exist.

One way in which we can understand more about that early universe is to simulate the conditions that existed at the time. Particle accelerators can help us to do this, by subjecting subatomic particles to conditions of intense energy and seeing what kinds of new particles are formed. But no particle accelerator in existence today can produce the concentration of energy that existed immediately after the Big Bang.

In fact, no accelerator that we could *ever* build would simulate such conditions, but if we can produce even a substantial fraction of that kind of energy, it may help physicists to revise their theories sufficiently to catch a glimpse of the ultimate nature of the universe. Such an experiment would expand our knowledge immensely.

The United States government has recently committed to building the largest particle accelerator ever, one capable of producing huge amounts of energy. It is called the *superconducting supercollider* (SSC) because it uses superconducting magnets. The SSC will be built in the form of a fifty-two mile (eighty-four kilometer) long, race-track-shaped tunnel, slightly larger than the island of Manhattan. In fact, the SSC was planned even before the discovery of high-temperature superconductors. It is designed to use low-temperature superconductors that are cooled with liquid helium.

However, some people have now suggested that the project be halted until it can be redesigned around the new high-temperature superconductors. It is argued that this will make the SSC cheaper to build and cheaper to run.

Other physicists, who believe that the SSC is too important to put back on the drawing board at this late date, argue that superconductor cooling costs are not very high compared to the overall costs of the supercollider and that there is no point in waiting for further superconductor developments. When *The New York Times* printed an editorial suggesting that the project be delayed, several well-known physicists (including John Bardeen and Robert Schrieffer of BCS theory fame) wrote letters of protest.

"The high temperature superconductors are in the very early research stage," argued Bardeen and Schrieffer. "While research is

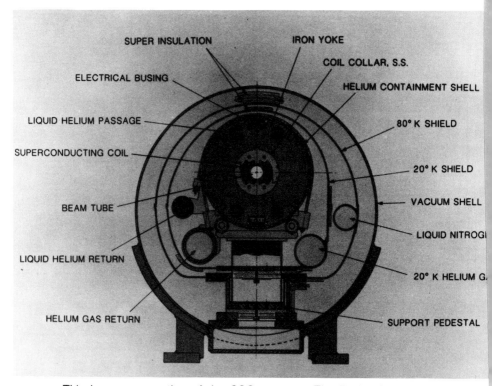

This is a cross-section of the SSC magnet. The liquid nitrogen cools the superconducting coil, whose magnetic fields then propel subatomic particles through the beam tube.

proceeding rapidly, many questions must be resolved before it is known whether or not they can be used in such applications as high-field superconducting magnets" (*The New York Times*, May 14, 1987).

At the current time, it seems unlikely that the SSC will contain high-temperature superconductors. However, Nobel laureate physicist Philip W. Anderson believes that the new superconductors will eventually be used to build a machine as powerful as the SSC, but only a tenth as big as the monstrously large supercollider.

Other Applications

In this chapter, we have seen only a glimpse of what the future may hold for high-temperature superconductors. Perhaps many of the most exciting applications for these substances will be ones that nobody has thought of yet. Superconductors are such a fundamental scientific breakthrough that we may need some time to fully work out the implications of their discovery.

For instance, researchers at Cornell University have discovered that superconductors can be used to make bearings, tiny spheres used to reduce friction between moving machine parts. Using the Meissner effect (see Chapter 2), superconducting bearings can actually float in the air—and thus are subject to almost no friction at all. A superconducting bearing may be able to rotate as many as one million times per minute in the absence of air. This is an application for superconductors that few people would have expected.

It is important to remember, though, that there are still many details to be worked out and problems to be overcome before the new high-temperature superconductors can be put to use. In the next chapter, we will look at these problems in more detail.

5

Obstacles and Opportunities

High-temperature superconductors are a major scientific breakthrough, but the road to creating the applications discussed in the previous chapter will be a bumpy one. There are many problems yet to be worked out before superconductors become common.

Not Warm Enough?

For one thing, the new high-temperature superconductors still need to be refrigerated. While the change from liquid helium cooling to liquid nitrogen cooling is an important one, it is still more than a little inconvenient to immerse superconductor devices in frigid liquid in order to make them work. Refrigerated home computers, for instance, are not likely to be very popular. Neither are superconducting electric cars. These and other applications will await the breakthrough to room-temperature superconductors—and no one knows yet whether such a breakthrough is even possible.

In the days and weeks after Paul Chu's announcement of superconductivity at 90 K, the scientific community was hopeful that room-temperature superconductivity was just around the corner. By

Scientists are working hard to make room-temperature superconductors a common part of life.

the end of the year, however, that enthusiasm had cooled considerably. The second burst of discovery that followed in the first months of 1988 renewed that enthusiasm, but it is unlikely that room-temperature superconductors will be available in the immediate future.

Not Strong Enough?

Another problem is that the new superconductors, while they may lack electrical resistance, are not very good at carrying strong electric currents. This may seem contradictory, but it is the case. High-temperature superconductors do a very good job of carrying weak currents, but many of them become normal conductors when subjected to a particularly strong current.

The highest current that the first high-temperature superconductors could carry was about 10 amps per square centimeter of wire (amps being a measure of current), which is about 1/1,000 of the current needed to run a powerful electromagnet. This is definitely a problem. Fortunately, even this small amount of current is adequate for certain devices, such as the Josephson junctions in a SQUID (which is why SQUIDs were among the first devices based on low-temperature superconductors to become commercially available).

In May 1987, however, the IBM Corporation announced that its scientists had learned how to make a high-temperature superconducting film that retained its superconductivity while carrying a current of 100,000 amps per square centimeter, more than adequate to run a powerful electromagnet. Subsequent experiments have pushed this limit even higher, into the millions of amps.

Not Flexible Enough?

Another problem that has hovered over the new superconductors is the question of wiring. To use these superconductors in many applications, such as power transport and electromagnets, the

This SQUID is used to measure the Meissner effect in high-temperature superconducting material.

superconductors will have to be formed into wires. But how do you make a wire out of a ceramic?

Until now, most conductors in commercial use have been metals. Metals are flexible, malleable, and easily shaped into wires. Those wires can be coiled, folded, even tied into knots. But a ceramic wire—in theory, at least—would be extremely brittle. How could you coil it to make an electromagnet? How could you bend it to carry electricity from the living room to the kitchen? One possibility is to bend the superconducting wire before the ceramic is heated, while it is still flexible. However, this will be of little comfort to people using superconducting wires in their homes, since such wires have lost their flexibility.

A number of groups, including both large corporations and university research laboratories, are working on the problem of making a flexible superconducting wire from existing superconductive ceramics and may succeed in the near future. If not, it is possible that other types of high-temperature superconductor may prove better suited for the manufacture of flexible wires. This would be an ideal application for a superconducting plastic, for instance, if such a substance can ever be found.

Will It Really Work?

There is also doubt as to the feasibility of some of the applications we discussed in the last chapter. Maglevs, for instance, may be technically possible but not economically feasible. In the United States, trains were long ago superseded by other forms of transportation: airplanes for long trips, automobiles for short trips, trucks for hauling cargo. Is there any reason to suppose that superconducting maglevs will revive public interest in riding trains?

Furthermore, it is possible to build levitating trains with ordinary magnets as well, and there is some evidence that such trains work as well as—or better than—those made from superconductors. But the operation of the magnets may be more costly without

Superconducting ceramic wires may be difficult to use commercially since they lose their flexibility when they are fired.

resistance-free superconductors to keep electric current swirling through their coils. So high-temperature superconductors may win out after all.

The Josephson junction has also come in for its share of criticism. JJs made from low-temperature superconductors perform well, though they are expensive and awkward to use. JJs made from high-temperature superconductors may not perform at all for any purpose more electrically demanding than a SQUID, which uses extremely low levels of power.

The problem is that Josephson junctions need low temperatures for reasons other than keeping their superconductive layers cooled. High temperatures—77 K, for instance—produce "background noise" inside the circuit, the noise of particles bouncing around with the vibrations of heat. This noise may be sufficient to render the junction completely inoperative. Thus, there may not be any point in making Josephson junctions out of high-temperature superconductors, since they may need to be refrigerated to 4 K just to remove the background noise. This problem does not bother the JJ chips in a SQUID because of its extremely small electrical requirements.

A final problem lies in the ability of superconductors to transmit currents over a long distance. Most of the excitement over superconductors comes from their ability to carry an electrical current without resistance—this, of course, is the very definition of a superconductor—but the kind of current that superconductors carry without resistance is *direct current*. The type of power used in the North American power system is *alternating current*—and superconductors cannot carry alternating current without loss of energy.

Should we switch from alternating current to direct current? Alternating current is the basis of our power system, and we have been using it for nearly a century. And large-scale direct current generation may not be feasible for other reasons as well. There is no immediate solution to this problem now, though perhaps, like other problems relating to superconductors, it will be solved through

The energy used in the North American power system is called alternating current.

sheer determination. When large sums of money are potentially involved, scientists can be surprisingly innovative.

The Future of Superconductivity

There is no reason to be discouraged by these problems and every reason to be encouraged by the future of superconductivity. Most or even all of these problems will probably be overcome in time. Many of the future applications discussed in the last chapter will eventually become reality. It is impossible to put a time limit on such technological changes—superfast home computers, for instance, may be available in five years or in fifty. But high-temperature superconductors will almost certainly become an integral part of our technology within the lifetimes of most readers of this book.

By early 1988, they had already become a commercial proposition. Powdered superconductors were already on sale, for the use of laboratories doing research into the substances, and were selling quite well. These versatile powders can be molded into many forms, or sprayed onto the surfaces of other substances.

Kits can also be purchased for demonstrating the Meissner effect in classrooms. These kits, available for about $50, consist of a superconducting ceramic and a magnet; with the addition of a small amount of inexpensive liquid nitrogen to cool the superconductor, the superconductor can be used to suspend the magneter in midair, as discussed in Chapter 2 of this book. The kits are supposedly quite popular, not only in schools but in the offices of businesses interested in superconductor technology.

Every now and then a scientific discovery comes along that changes our lives in varied and unexpected ways. The transistor was one such discovery: it gave us portable radios and Pacman, microcomputers and inexpensive color televisions. Much further back in time, the printing press also revolutionized the way we live, making knowledge available to the masses and changing their lives forever.

It is rarely possible to predict how such an invention will change our lives before the changes actually take place. Perhaps that will be the case with superconductors. Today we are wondering exactly what we will do with them; perhaps tomorrow we will wonder what we ever did without them.

Glossary

absolute zero - the lowest possible temperature, at which all (or almost all) motion of particles ceases; also called 0 Kelvin, -273° Celsius, and -459° Fahrenheit.

alternating current (AC) - an electric current in which the electrons constantly reverse their direction of movement.

atoms - the particles of which all materials are made.

Celsius - the metric temperature scale, with 0° equal to the freezing point of water and 100° equal to the boiling point of water.

ceramic - substance made out of materials raised to a high temperature and then cooled until they harden.

conductor - a substance with an atomic structure that allows the free flow of electrons.

Cooper pairs - pairs of electrons in a superconductor that behave like a single particle, which is not subject to the electrical resistance experienced by unpaired electrons.

crystalline - describes a substance in which the atomic structure is extremely regular and latticelike.

direct current (DC) - an electric current in which the electrons move continuously in the same direction.

electric charge - a special property of certain kinds of subatomic particles.

electric circuit - a loop of conducting material in which electricity can flow in a continuous circle.

electric current - the flow of electrons.

electromagnet - a magnet created by running an electric current through a coil of conducting wire.

electron - one of the particles that make up the atom; the smallest component of an electric current.

element - a substance made up of a single kind of atom.

Fahrenheit - the temperature scale commonly used in the United States by nonscientists.

fusion - see *nuclear fusion*.

high-temperature superconductors - substances that become superconductive at temperatures of 77 K or higher, allowing them to be cooled by relatively inexpensive liquid nitrogen.

insulator - a substance with an atomic structure that does not allow the free flow of electrons; a nonconductor.

ions - atoms that have gained or lost electrons and thereby gained an overall electric charge.

Josephson effect - a phenomenon in which an electric current passing through a current produces radio waves (and vice versa); discovered by Brian Josephson.

Josephson junction - high-speed electronic circuit that utilizes the Josephson effect for transmitting signals.

Kelvin - a temperature scale that begins at absolute zero.

low-temperature superconductor - a substance that becomes a superconductor when lowered to a temperature close to absolute zero.

maglev - *mag*netically *lev*itated train; a train that is suspended above its tracks on a magnetic field.

magnetic bottle - method of confining hot gases during nuclear fusion.

magnetic field - the area around the magnet in which it exerts forces on other magnetically charged substances.

magnetometer - a device for measuring the strength of very small magnetic fields.

Meissner effect - the tendency of a superconductor to exclude (that is, repel) a magnetic field.

metals - elements in which electrons tend to move about freely within the matrix of atoms.

negative - one type of electric charge, the opposite of positive.

neutrons - subatomic particles found in the nucleus of atoms, except for the hydrogen atom.

noble gases - a type of element the atoms of which do not tend to bond with other atoms.

nonconductor - see *insulator*.

north pole - one end of a magnet; opposite of the south pole.

nuclear fusion - method of generating power by fusing hot hydrogen atoms together into helium atoms.

nucleus - the central portion of an atom, consisting of neutrons and protons.

particle accelerator - machine for accelerating subatomic particles to high speeds similar to those experienced in the first seconds after the creation of the universe.

particle beam weapon (PBW) - a proposed weapon to shoot down missiles by shooting subatomic particles at them to scramble their guidance systems.

phonon - a vibration in the atomic lattice of an electrical conductor.

positive - one type of electric charge, the opposite of negative.

protons - subatomic particles found in the nucleus of atoms.

resistance - the tendency of a substance not to conduct electricity.

room-temperature superconductors - substances that are superconductive at room temperature, so that they do not require expensive and bulky cooling equipment to maintain.

shell - the region in which an electron moves around the nucleus of an atom.

south pole - one end of a magnet; opposite of the north pole.

SQUID - *s*uperconducting *qu*antum *i*nterference *d*evice; device for measuring the strength of extremely small magnetic fields.

Strategic Defense Initiative (SDI) - program initiated by the Reagan administration to develop a space-based defense against nuclear weapons; popularly known as Star Wars.

subatomic particles - particles that are smaller than atoms.

superconducting supercollider (SSC) - a giant particle accelerator to be built by the United States in the 1990s; if constructed, it will be the largest such accelerator ever built.

superconductor - a substance that conducts electricity without resistance.

transition temperature - the temperature below which a substance becomes a superconductor.

Further Reading

Catherall, Ed. *Magnets and Magnetism*. Morristown, New Jersey: Silver Burdett, 1972.

Chester, Michael. *Particles: An Introduction to Particle Physics*. New York: Macmillan, 1978.

Gutnik, Martin J. *Simple Electrical Devices*. New York: Franklin Watts, 1986.

Lampton, Christopher. *Fusion: The Eternal Flame*. New York: Franklin Watts, 1982.

———. *Star Wars*. New York: Franklin Watts, 1987.

Leon, George deLucenay. *The Electricity Story: 2,500 Years of Experiments and Discoveries*. New York: Arco, 1983.

Math, Irwin. *Wires & Watts: Understanding and Using Electricity*. New York: Scribners, 1981.

Index

91

About the Author

Christopher Lampton is a widely published author of science books for young people. Although he is interested in many scientific subjects, he especially enjoys working with and learning about computers.